From the Depth of This Journey

poems by

Isabel Huston

Finishing Line Press
Georgetown, Kentucky

From the Depth of This Journey

"The light of love is always in us, no matter how cold the flame. It is always present waiting for the spark to ignite, waiting for the heart to awaken and call us back to the first memory of being the life force inside a dark place waiting to be born—waiting to see the light."
—bell hooks, All About Love

For all the lights in my life who refuse to let me stop shining. I am because you are.

Copyright © 2020 by Isabel Huston
ISBN 978-1-64662-330-3 First Edition
All rights reserved under International and Pan-American Copyright Conventions. No part of this book may be reproduced in any manner whatsoever without written permission from the publisher, except in the case of brief quotations embodied in critical articles and reviews.

ACKNOWLEDGMENTS

Thank you to all the women who are so instrumental in these experiments with testing my wings. I am so grateful for your faith in me. Your ability to see my strengths makes it possible for me to share my words with the world. Special thanks to Rebecca Weiss Roberts, Lauren Valentino, Gillian Winkler, Grace Woodruff Diaz, Diana Christian, Alison Friedman Philips, Mai-Trang Dang, Udeitha Srimushnam, Dani Fishman, and Allison Conyers-Mooring for taking the time to read my drafts and providing feedback along the way. To Pauline Arneberg for helping me find the courage to want more for myself. To Terri Solomon and all those involved with the YouthInk! competition at McCarter Theatre in Princeton for giving me the audacious idea so long ago that I have things to say that people need to hear. And to my parents, for the love and art supplies and encouragement and space to be myself. And to Cal, without you this never could have happened. Thank you.

Publisher: Leah Huete de Maines
Editor: Christen Kincaid
Cover Art: Isabel Huston
Author Photo: Mai-Trang Dang
Cover Design: Elizabeth Maines McCleavy

Order online: www.finishinglinepress.com
also available on amazon.com

Author inquiries and mail orders:
Finishing Line Press
P. O. Box 1626
Georgetown, Kentucky 40324
U. S. A.

Table of Contents

Pacific Surfliner 1
From India with Love 4
Now Pre-boarding 5
A Woman 6
First 7
Valkyries 8
City of Palms 9
Street Music 10
Mantra 12
Champlain 13
This Garden 14
Princess 15
Mute 16
Overwhelmed 17
Collision 18
Fencepost 19
November 21
Shock and Awe 22
Keep the Mug 23
Sirens 25
Moonscape 26
Velvet Bird 27
It Goes On 28
Traveling Heart 29
Snake Poem 30
Daddy's Girl 31
Thirty-One 32
Memorial Service 33
Letter to My Dear One 34

Pacific Surfliner

The harbor and the sky are a riot of clashing blues
Boats snugly rocking
Telling shushing secrets in the
Knock knock of their hulls
Echoed in the rock rock of train wheels on parallel tracks
Knock knock
Rock rock
We are off

Alternating chaparral and Ocean
Sweeping Pacific views hoarded to reward
That sweet Protestant Work Ethic
Killing us all
But at least we had a house at the beach

Waves on waves on waves
And surfers dotting the shore
This state where people make use of the sunshine
Hustling over sidewalks and dirt tracks
Hungrily growing golden and thin
Everyone has a dog

A man takes out the garbage in a trailer park.
Wiry thin, covered in tattoos.
We ought to set more tragedies in Southern California
So many people ran away to the gold rush
—To the endless blue sky and cheer—
Only to realize they couldn't leave themselves behind
At least in the East the close grey cold
Makes our difficulties expected

Military base or prison?
Hard to tell from this moving window picaresque
Barbed wire surrounds so many of our institutions i
ts meaning is all but lost
Is it keeping outsiders out or insiders in?

Giant American flag flops in the sea breeze at the center of the compound
It is not a clue at all
Every one of us prisoners of our own idealized Freedom

The beach is a home and a state of mind
with every passing lifeguard stand
I am increasingly confused about what
I've been trying to build
Let it wash away like a sand castle in the break
Give it up to the tide
Submerge in the salt and the brine

Tracks curve away from the water
(Heartbreak!)
To the right snow-capped mountains
Every scene here a gift
In California they have too much
Yet life, in its everydayness, still manages to be mundane

Wild orange trees in a field of goldenrod
Unattended but so deeply significant
Did anyone else see? Did they understand?
Did tears sting their eyes too?
The vitality and color of it all
How could your soul not move?

The home of Angels and Ducks and everything Disneyfied swings into view
The land thickly developed
Concrete buildings fell here, landing fully formed from the sky

Get me back to the East Coast
Moldering old homes crowding sinister, winding streets
The cobbles are old and the ghosts, lost on their way home, are stuck in the corners
Generations growing on top of one another
Cities like spliced trees: one thing full of bizarre new growth
History's bony hands do not grip these wide and sunwashed boulevards the same

The snow in the mountains is vital
The sky is powdered electricity
Nothing threatening about midwinter here
And I do not have enough time left alone

This is the final stop
Everything in Los Angeles
Feels both new and like the set of an old western
Dress code high stakes casual
And the hills, with their lingering wildness create a cap that hold
Our dreams within reach

From India with Love

This love bloomed overnight
Sweet as the lilies, deep and cool
Overtook me like a wave
The ones that crashed on the rocks
While you held me
And we watched the sun creep closer
To the horizon
Our time, connection, limited to those
Daylight hours

Your sweet eyes bore down
Clay-red drills cracking barriers
Erected over years
Sending me back around the globe
A raw and leaking mess
Arriving at customs to declare myself
Softened, no longer afraid of bruising

I opened at the close
Soon enough for you to catch the tears in my eyelashes
With your lips
Too late to be healed

Now Pre-boarding

Alone at the airport again
In that quiet moment at the gate
Between the harrowing rush at security
And the calm of being unreachable, literally above it all
Melancholy returns
Thinking of a man
Made of marble
Thought I could pull him from the stone
(Naïveté made Arthur a King, after all)
Not understanding his objective
To keep this form:
Cold and unmoved
Pulling warmth by osmosis
From the living
So persistently, greedily cool
I am flying 3000 miles away
To warm up

A Woman

My body
Gets in the way
Of your ability
To See me

A woman

First

"No"

Pain

Blood on a leg

Trickles to the floor

(Blood, always with us women
So shameful to be us
That our insides
Are constantly trying to escape)

Valkyries

They never thought to count
All the shattered women
Until we made
Shields of our broken hearts
And became warriors

City of Palms

At the end of the known world
Sun on the brain
We are beautiful and reckless
Heart wild energy
Glowing untouchable
Golden

Street Music

You've got some nice eyes
Hey girl, where'd you get them thighs?
Honk, Honk
Beep, Beep
One long, high whistle
And a symphony of catcalls

This is the feeling of female meat
This is the music of the street

Persistent and overplayed
Love music, lust music
I am not a fan of the beat

Nice eyes
Nice ass
Butterscotch, give me a hug
Do you like horses?
Then come on baby, take me for a ride
I had been looking to get myself a wife…

No thank you, but have a nice night
Dance to the music
Sidestep; move back, eyes on the floor
This is not flattering anymore

You should be dancing
You should be dancing with me
(and I don't care if you're tired, get that fine ass on the floor)

Turn down the stereo
Shut and lock the door
Take a deep breath and fall away
I don't need more sex appeal
More lewd music on the street

I'm not much for that overeager beat
No more nighttime hellos,
Early morning goodbyes
No more speculation on my thighs
Give me a solo violin
Strong, confident and finely tuned
A virtuoso making perfect music on its own
Or a duet in perfect thirds
The simple harmony of a lasting warm embrace
No more clichéd sampling of lines
No more auto tune; voices fake, generic
Give me something real
Give me something to make me feel

Mantra

I love my whole being
Every piece of this full softness

Champlain

There is no sound like
The peeling of still water
Right at the ears
A thousand china dinner plates
Lovingly shattered
Right at the eardrum
Tiny, tinkling, tears
It is love
Peace of unknown proportions
Gifted to a lone swimmer
Submerged to the ears in a gemstone lake

This Garden

Love, they forget to tell you,
When left unattended
With nowhere to go
Grows persistently
—And fast—
In the chest
Choking everything
Rooting in the heart
Setting forth through the chest cavity
It loops around the lungs—a floral boa constrictor
Decorates the ribs like ivy
(The classic illusion of sophistication…
Until you notice the roots are desiccating the structure underneath)
Love, untended, crowds the diaphragm; compresses the voice box
Love, a weed, flowering and pernicious
Conquers without a gardener
Is not always welcome to propagate

Princess

Do not call me beautiful
As if it is a secret password
Such easy praise does not make you
A valiant knight
Come to release some imagined damsel
Forced to spend her good years
Locked away, nothing to do but smooth her hair

I like the frizz
And we both know
I slayed that dragon years ago

Mute

There are so many words
I cannot speak

The nasty ones want to
Crawl into your ear, sting you like
Yellow jackets
Your hands, tongue
Crown me Queen of the Universe
This hot breath wants
To tear you apart

The soft words want to roost
On each of your eyelashes
In the quiet and
Swan dive into that overwhelming mind

The sincere ones uttered in intimate moments
(Before we ruined it with fucking)
Sit on the windowsill,
Our starving children tossed off
In favor of desire

I would speak you into existence
Were I brave or strong
If words could build a track across
The desert of your hurt to find youd
Heart still mending
I would speak them all

Overwhelmed

Forgive the staring
A million thoughts rushed
To my mouth
At the sight of your lips
My tongue is buried

Collision

I want
I want and I want and I want
Your hands
Smile
Eyes locked
Wrong side of the bed
To tear your chest open and
Wrap my fingers around your heart
To slam into you at such a rate
That our minds hearts tears
Become one
The warmth of your skin and cold of
Your trauma
Intermingling with mine

Fencepost

A pile of paper scraps, autumn leaves
Carefully corralled on the sidewalk
Is only a pile
Subject to the gusting of crisp, cool, changing winds
Vulnerable to scattering separation
Disintegration biodegradation

Carefully cut puzzle pieces
Lying haphazard in their box
Are nothing without care
Bits lost forever
Underneath the chair
On the screened porch of the lakehouse
Taken by gravity
The whole forever incomplete
Picture always marred

Humans are the same
A random amalgam of
Thought feeling want need idea
With the right force our contents are scattered
Across space, time, experience

Tie tie me down
Protect these parts
Skin to skin
Back to front
Keep me on the ground

A lost balloon floats
String cut from a child's wrist
Unintelligible dot in the sky
Where will it go? How far will it fly?
Contents slowly leaking along its
Buffeted path
To arrive deflated on a distant shore
(or tangled, torn, in the branches of a neighbor's tree)

A tree without roots falls unfed
A book without binding misplaces its plot
Bind my being to the ground
Protect this purpose
Compress these manias
Arm to hip
Thigh to thigh
My humanity in your eyes
Slow my colors' fade

Fence post paper weight be here now
Earthly reminder
Tie tie me down
To keep me here.

November

The year beginning to end
Trees releasing their leaves
Dropping, forgotten summer decoration not needed
In the shortening light

Preparing to refer to these present
Moments in past tense

The Russians have a word
For that feeling of nostalgia
Toward things we have not yet left:
Toska

Apt for those living
Where the days are constantly ending

When the wind blows down my collar
Nips at the ankles
(Reminds me to wear socks next time)
I feel all of that for us

Shock and Awe

The most spectacular disappointments
Are fireworks displays
Surreally executed
And awe inspiring

They captivate you with color, discovery
Oohs and Ahs roll at the utterance
Of every detail

Explosions—though you may try to prepare for them—
Shudder deep in the chest, move the ground you assumed solid

When it's over
The sound gone, precious stillness returned
The sky obscured, grey and sulfurous
We are left alone

To realize that the shock has left a pressure,
Ringing in our ears,
That defines the shape of the skull

We carry the show home to bed
Hoping to wake whole again
Though the experience, consumed,
Is ever within us now

Keep the Mug

In a moment of post-coital generosity
I told you to take the Shakespearean Insults Mug
That was a gift from my brother two Christmases ago
You were so enamoured of it, and I mistook relinquishing some clutter for
Growth
Not realizing the thing I ought to be letting go
Was you

Now it's been so long
I cannot wash you from my mind
It would be easier to clean that mug of coffee stains

Over and again
I write you out
And write you out
Out! (Out, damn spot!)
You are the The Lady not a prince
Though I've seen you wear a crown of blood
Did you wash this Witch out of your mouth upon returning home?

Hamlet suits you better, friend,
(There is something rotten, I know)
Wise, old, young, fool
Does your father haunt your mirrors, too?
Don't worry about me,
I would always rather sail for adventure
with Rosencrantz and Guildenstern
Than drown myself in melodrama
Awaiting your return

A midsummer night's dream it started
Sunny, humid sorcery
Titania I wish to be, Helena is how you see me
But woke in the Autumn to find myself Puck: The Unsuspecting Ass
You silver-tongued Hyperion
You cad you trickster
Pick a phrase from that mug, you perjured, false, disloyal man

Any high school English class teaches us:
Tragedy and comedy are close cousins
(It's why I laughed in your face where I ought to have cried)
You beautiful, peripatetic, inconsistent boor
It wasn't even worth the effort to make you watch me go mad

Insecure, you needed a prop
So everyone would know you: A Writer
But I have to tell you, I'm not convinced Shakespeare got anything right.
There's nothing to be learned from Romeo and Juliet but pettiness and impetuous death
Sonnets are stand ins for soft core porn
(It's a wonder you've not written me one, given this delicious aromantic tryst)
And can we get any empathy for the Shrew?
Who might she have become had those men not set out to tame her?

As You Like It
I am not Viola, won't disguise myself to please a man
Keep the mug
And though the opportunity for powerful mischief abounds
I will stay the spirits, calm the seas to send you on
To Tunis (and a wedding near as hasty as Miranda and Ferdinand)
I have my books and spells and this sterling wit to keep me company

Sirens

Sirens lie in wait for you,
Young man,
Have known your kind long before
Those sails broke the horizon
The winds were always blowing
toward this:
peremptory, desirous, vengeance

Look straight ahead and pretend control
(As if sailing were ever linear)
Lash your body to the mast
Tie a blindfold to your eyes
Stuff your ears with cotton
Pledge you won't dive headlong for the waves

But we know the siren song
Is already inside
Your weak and wanton core
As far as you may go
You'll return
To have that body torn apart
Upon this shore

Moonscape

Passing time
What was once "could be"
Becomes "didn't evolve"
Fondness fomenting ferments
This new iteration a gentle poison
Extended silence a river of broken glass
Shards passing on a current formed of
The Gulf Between
Action and inaction reminds
That the backside of the heart
Is cold and dark as the far side of the moon

Velvet Bird

I cannot keep Anger in my body
It rises and rages and fans and flames
A living being
A devil bird

A flying raptor hatched in the stomach
Flapping clumsy infant wings
Rolling roiling rising

A bonfire heats in the throat
Escaping with a gasp and a cry
Disturbing the air
Silent chaos rule this room
Everything smells like sulfur

Hollow, nauseous in separation
The things I failed to say leave
A heavy mouthful of ashes
Pinning my head to the pillow
Staring at the ceiling wondering when
I'll forget your crimes
Longing for you to appear again

I am distracted and Anger,
That large bird
Slips through a draft at the windowsill
And joins the wandering, anxious, lonely
Soul birds texturing the velveteen city night

It Goes On

The beautiful thing about
Getting older (not old, no, just older)
Is that the voice in the pit of our stomachs
Right there next at the center (next to the dread and the worry and the shame)
Gets louder and stronger and more certain

Until its mantra becomes a drumbeat
Driving us through the anger and the doubt and the pain
"Life goes on. Life goes on. Life goes on."

Get up, tie your shoes, open the door
Though you have to cradle that broken heart
Crushed upon the floor

Life goes on, my dear
On and on in beauty and despair
Through hill and dale in breathtaking and sharp detail

Life goes on
Life goes on
Life goes on

Traveling Heart

My love sings and soars
Ever expanding velvet soft
Circumnavigating the globe
(Itinerant)

Lighting wooded paths
Diving, fearless, from mountain tops
Floating in the cold depths of gemstone colored lakes
Lodged at the roots of thick, tall trees (those quiet, constant, sentinels)

My heart lives and grows
In the wild
For the hearts of men
Have proven too fickle and small
To hold it

Snake Poem

When they have outgrown
A moment in time
Snakes shed their skins
Leaving too small husks
On the forest floor

(Evidence of prior manifestations for
We the Nostalgic to stumble upon
Conjuring visions of our own, smaller selves)

Uncaring, our serpentine friends
Cruise on
Longer, yet still the same
Growing room for their next iteration
At every moment

We bipeds, though,
Get one form
A set amount of cubic inches
Wherein we pack
Every version of ourselves
Crumpling memories into every vacant space

A heavy load, our multiplicity
It crowds the room where
Possibility would go

Daddy's Girl

In raising difficult daughters
Do fathers
Come to know more
Or less
Of women
Than when they were simply
Men?

Thirty-One

Ancient being
Connected to every soul
Each word familiar
Every wind that passes already
Blown before
Each sunset a callback to
Another closer to the time
When life began

Barefoot child never really released
Always wiggling toes in the dirt
To feel the pulse of All Eternal
At the core of this place

She is the stars and the moon
She is every infernal blade of grass
She is the sky in its spherical expanse
A witch, a queen, a prophet
A deep and watery heart
Constantly flooding its walls

Weary of the battle, yet
Girding for the next fight
She will endure and laugh and love
And spark the horizon with light

Memorial Service

Gone, though the forgetting began
Years ago
Before I knew what it was to be a woman
To excavate her from the rubble of the late years
Is to stare my own existence in the face
And hope it grows to its greatest fullness

A loss, well and truly
I didn't expect it to hurt so much
This sadness feels old and bigger than me
Do parts of our souls detach and regenerate
Like plant clippings, transferred from one generation to the next?
(mothers: philodendrons all)
Because parts of me feel abandoned viscerally

A shadow framed by North Country mountain sunlight
My memories of you are like looking through that screened porch door
Why were we never as connected as the sum of our love predicated?
Because everyone in our family fears women
Scotch and cigars on the porch
Outside space for the men to grow larger in the night breeze

I didn't know we shared this well of power
Warm and dark like our shared blood
until you were gone
And I felt it in my body
A loss…
I am sorry for it
I never knew the meaning of that phrase until now

I haven't worn those pearls in years
But I find myself returning to the closet
Slinging their cool roundness about my neck
To feel the weight of your life
Hung on my collarbones

Letter to My Dear One

Womanhood for so long seemed
Defined by confinement, constraint
A trap designed to keep
The wild winds of my world complacent
So I thought, I'd rather be a Wolf
Tough paws eating miles of tundra per day
Thoroughly shot through with the depth of the Earth
But even wolves return to a family den

Having come upon my first days of considering
How and if to carry a life
In me then with me
Forever
Never alone
Never just myself again
I wonder if the tragedy of womanhood is that we
Forfeit our identities in the name of the Next Generation
Just as we come into full focus
Dead in some ways before our youth takes its leave

My own life has been
A burden
How could I carry another name, heart, soul body
When I wake and feel suspicious of my own
So regularly?

I cannot convince you to join us,
Sweet One,
For I am not sure what any of us
Are doing here.

Isabel Huston is a writer, artist, coach, and facilitator living in Washington, DC. In her art and professional work she is dedicated to creating a stronger sense of connection between people, and a space for vulnerability to prosper. She holds a BA in English and Sociology from Wesleyan University and a Masters of Public Policy from The George Washington University. When she's not writing she works with leaders to help them find their power and voice in civic life and plays ice hockey.

www.ingramcontent.com/pod-product-compliance
Lightning Source LLC
LaVergne TN
LVHW041601070426
835507LV00011B/1224